HOLY WATER AND ITS
SIGNIFICANCE FOR CATHOLICS

Rev. Henry Theiler, S.O.Cist.

HOLY
WATER

❯❯—————————❮❮

and ITS SIGNIFICANCE
for CATHOLICS

SOPHIA INSTITUTE PRESS
Manchester, New Hampshire

Nihil obstat: Remigius LaFort, S.T.L., Censor
Imprimatur: John M. Farley, Archbishop of New York
New York, April 5, 1909

Sophia Institute Press
Box 5284, Manchester, NH 03108
1-800-888-9344

www.SophiaInstitute.com

Sophia Institute Press® is a registered trademark of Sophia Institute.

Library of Congress Cataloging-in-Publication Data

Names: Theiler, Heinrich, 1875- author.
Title: Holy water and its significance for Catholics / Rev. Henry Theiler, S.O.Cist.
Other titles: Weihwasser und seine Bedeutung für den katholischen Christen. English
Description: Manchester, New Hampshire : Sophia Institute Press, 2016. | Originally published: New York : Fr. Pustet and Company, 1909.
Identifiers: LCCN 2016011985 | ISBN 9781622823390 (pbk. : alk. paper)
Subjects: LCSH: Holy water.
Classification: LCC BX2307 .T5 2016 | DDC 247—dc23 LC record available at https://lccn.loc.gov/2016011985

First printing

CONTENTS

HOLY WATER AND ITS SIGNIFICANCE FOR CATHOLICS

"The first thing, O man, that you have to venerate, is the age of the waters in that their substance is ancient; the second, their dignity, in that they were the seat of the Divine Spirit, more pleasing to Him, no doubt, than all the other then existing elements. For the darkness was total thus far, shapeless, without the ornament of stars; and the abyss gloomy; and the earth unfurnished; and the heaven unwrought: water alone — always a perfect, gladsome, simple material substance, pure in itself — supplied a worthy vehicle to God."

TERTULLIAN
(B. 160)

"With water all things are washed and nourished, and cleansed and bedewed. Water bears the earth, water produces the dew, water exhilarates the vine; water matures the corn in the ear, water ripens the grape cluster, water softens the olive, water sweetens the palm-date, water reddens the rose and decks the violet, water makes the lily bloom with its brilliant cups. And why should I speak at length? Without the element of water, none of the present order of things can subsist.

So necessary is the element of water; for the other elements took their places beneath the highest vault of the heavens, but the nature of water obtained a seat also above the heavens. And to this the prophet himself is a witness, when he exclaims, "Praise the Lord, ye heavens of heavens, and the water that is above the heavens."

ST. HIPPOLYTUS
(D. 236)

Chapter 1

WATER'S SIGNIFICANCE IN NATURE AND GRACE

On the first page of Holy Writ we read that "the Spirit of God moved over the waters" (Gen. 1:2). Why did the spirit of God move over the waters? The writings of the Holy Doctors make reply: to bless them, that they might become adaptable to their task in the work of Creation. The holy apostle Peter thus briefly attests these tasks of the waters:

> For this they [deceitful scoffers] are willfully ignorant of, that the heavens were before, and the earth out of water, and through water, consisting by the word of God" (2 Pet. 3:5).

And, too, after Creation, water has an important function to perform in the realm of nature, and be it said, likewise in the realm of grace. Reflect for a moment how in nature every living creature requires water and how our springs and streams, carrying their blessings, spread over the land. They are to the soil what the circulation of the blood is to the human body. As the blood circulates from the heart throughout the body and returns, so rise the waters from the lakes, fructify the thirsty soil by refreshing rains, and return to the lakes and oceans.

And as water plays its important part in nature's kingdom, so too it does in the province of grace as the blessed and holy water.

The old Romans made use of a water that they held sacred. We are told by Ovid, Virgil, and Cicero of a sacred water with which the people, the homes, and the fields were sprinkled, that by this sprinkling plagues might be warded off and the stains of sin wiped away.

"Christ, the Maker of all, came down as the rain, and was known as a spring, and diffused Himself as a river, and was baptized in the Jordan. Oh, things strange beyond compare! How should the boundless River that makes glad the city of God have been dipped in a little water! The illimitable Spring that bears life to all men, and has no end, was covered by poor and temporary waters! He who is present everywhere, and absent nowhere—who is incomprehensible to angels and invisible to men—comes to the baptism according to His own good pleasure. The Spirit appeared as a Dove over the waters of the Jordan on that day, thereby making the symbolic connection between water and Spirit complete."

ST. HIPPOLYTUS
(D. 236)

The Christian writer Tertullian, who lived in the second century, tells us that the heathens made use of a holy water and ascribed to it the power not only of washing away bodily uncleanliness but also of wiping out sin.

Among the Jews, blessed water had a particular signification. They had special laws for the use of the so-called water of aspersion. For instance, "he that toucheth the corpse of a man, and is therefore unclean seven days, shall be sprinkled with this water on the third day, and on the seventh, and so shall be cleansed" (Num. 19:11–12).

And not only were such persons to be sprinkled with this water, but also their dwellings and their furniture. "And a man that is clean shall dip hyssop in it, and shall sprinkle therewith all the tent, and all the furniture, and the men that are defiled" (Num. 19:18). So important was this sprinkling that anyone who was defiled "and not sprinkled with this mixture, shall profane the tabernacle of the Lord, and shall perish out of Israel, because he was not sprinkled with the water of expiation" (Num. 19:13).

It is evident that this expiation was not a cleansing from sin, for it can certainly not be held a sin to confer upon the dead a corporal work of mercy. Holy Writ praises the good Tobias because he buried the dead (Tob. 12:12). But because death is a consequence of sin, and in a measure bears with it the stain of sin, and because God would make plain to the Israelites the malice of sin, He ordained that all who came in contact with a corpse, and thus likewise with death, thus in a certain measure too became contaminated with the stain of sin, should be held corporally unclean. And from this uncleanliness should the Jews become cleansed by holy water.

The sacred water of heathen use, of which mention has been made, is the foreshadowing of the waters of expiation used by the Jews and likewise a foreshadowing of the sacred waters that we Catholics know as holy water.

The use of holy water comes to us, in the Catholic Church, with all that is in its favor, even from the Old Testament. It signifies now, as then, cleansing, as did the ablutions commanded in the old law, by Almighty God, down to the baptism by John in Jordan's waters. Who would gainsay that our Lord used water for this same purpose when washing the disciples' feet on the eve of His suffer-ings? And again, He made water a condition necessary for salvation: "Unless a man be born again of water he cannot enter the Kingdom of Heaven" (John 3:5).

Holy water has been used in the Church as it is now, through the centuries, back to the

Apostles' days. It is spoken of in the *Apostolic Constitutions*. Pope Alexander, who died in the year 130, in his pontifical decree confirming this apostolic tradition says: "We bless salt and water for the people, that all who may be sprinkled therewith may be cleansed and sanctified."

The martyr St. Justin, who died in the year 163, tells us that the faithful in his time were sprinkled in their assemblies with Holy Water every Sunday. So too we find Holy Water mentioned in St. Cyprian's writings in the third century, in the works of St. Basil in the fourth, in the writings of St. Jerome in the fifth, and by St. Gregory the Great in the sixth century.

"Wherever Christ is, there is water: He Himself is baptized in water; when called to a marriage He inaugurates with water the first rudiments of His power; when engaged in conversation He invites those who are athirst to come to His everlasting water; when teaching of charity He approves of a cup of water offered to a little one as one of the works of affection; He walks upon the water; by His own choice He crosses over the water; with water He makes Himself a servant to His disciples. He continues His witness to Baptism right on to His Passion: when He is given up to the Cross, water is in evidence, as Pilate's hands are aware; when He receives a wound water bursts forth from His side, as the soldier's spear can tell."

TERTULLIAN

Chapter 2

———✦———

Holy Water Is
a Sacramental

Holy water is one of the sacramentals, which are things made sacred by rites of the Church in the manner of Christ. In the Catholic Church we have sacrament and sacramentals. These latter differ from the sacraments. Christ our Lord gave us the sacraments. The Church, exercising the authority He gave her, instituted the sacramentals.

They differ also in this: the sacraments of themselves, upon worthy reception, confer the particular grace that Christ attached to each of them; the sacramentals do not confer but obtain grace, as does, for instance, prayer.

Those who make use of them in a pious disposition have great advantages from them. They incite piety and thus cause the remission of venial sins. They likewise cause the remission of temporal punishments due to sin. They put to flight and stay the power of the devil. They obtain bodily health and other temporal benefits. These blessings follow as the effects of the prayers of the Church that are used in blessing and consecrating the sacramentals.

All religious rites and sacred things used in administering the sacraments are sacramentals; as for instance, the holy oils, blessed salt, holy water, and the Sign of the Cross.

Although some of the sacraments are necessary for salvation, we cannot claim this for the sacramentals. Consequently, holy water is not necessary for salvation. But although it is not thus necessary, it is beneficial and helpful. To ascertain this still better we will consider the effects flowing from the pious use of holy water. These effects may best be learned from the prayers pronounced by the priest in blessing the water.

"Blessed are you, Lord, Almighty God,
who deigned to bless us in Christ,
the living water of our salvation,
and to reform us interiorly.
Grant that we who are fortified
by the sprinkling of or use of this water,
the youth of the spirit being renewed
by the power of the Holy Spirit,
may walk always in newness of life."

THE *NOVUS ORDO*
BLESSING OF WATER

Chapter 3

BLESSING THE WATER

Holy water consists of a mixture of blessed salt and blessed water. The priest, as the minister of the Church, first blesses salt that he afterward puts into the water.

The blessing of salt and the casting of it into the water is following the example of the prophet Eliseus (Elisha), who by God's command took salt and cast it into the unwholesome waters of Jericho and made them good.

> And the men of the city said to Eliseus: Behold the situation of this city is very good, as thou my Lord seest; but the waters are very bad, and the ground barren. And he said: Bring me a new vessel,

and put salt into it. And when they had brought it, he went out to the spring of the waters, cast the salt into it and said: Thus saith the Lord: I have healed these waters, and there shall be no more in them death or barrenness. And the waters were healed unto this day, according to the word of Eliseus which he spoke. (4 Kings 2:19–20)[1]

Calling upon God's assistance, the priest, making upon himself the Sign of the Cross, says: "Our help is in the name of the Lord, who hath made heaven and earth."

Thereupon he pronounces a prayer over the salt to free it from the curse that God pronounced upon Creation as a consequence of Adam's sin. By this curse Satan gained power over creatures, and he seeks thereby also to

[1] RSV = 2 Kings 2:19–22.

harm mankind. This power of Satan is now to
be broken, so that he may no longer be able to
exercise power over this salt. The priest spreads
his hand over the salt and pronounces the following prayer:

> Our help is in the name of the Lord, who
> hath made heaven and earth. I exorcise
> thee, thou creature salt, by the living God,
> by the true God, by the holy God, by the
> God who commanded thee to be cast into
> the water by Eliseus, the prophet, that
> the sterility of the water might be healed,
> that thou mayest become salt exorcised
> unto the healing of the faithful; that thou
> mayest become health of soul and body
> to all who take thee; that every delusion
> and wickedness and snare of diabolical
> cunning and every unclean spirit may
> depart from the place in which thou shalt

be sprinkled, when adjured by Him who is to come to judge the living and the dead and the world by fire. Amen.

Let us pray. We humbly implore Thy boundless clemency, almighty and ever-lasting God, that of Thy bounty Thou wouldst deign to bless and sanctify this creature salt, which Thou hast given for the use of mankind; let it be unto all who take it health of mind and body; that whatsoever shall be touched or sprinkled with it be freed from all man-ner of uncleanness, and from all assaults of spiritual wickedness. Through our Lord Jesus Christ, who liveth and reigneth with Thee in the unity of the Holy Spirit forever. Amen.

In the following prayer the blessing is pro-nounced over the water:

I exorcise thee, O creature water, in the name of God the Father Almighty, and in the name of Jesus Christ, His Son, our Lord; and in the power of the Holy Spirit; that Thou mayest become water exorcised for the chasing away of all the power of the enemy; that thou mayest have strength to uproot and cast out the enemy himself and his apostate angels, by the power of the same, our Lord Jesus Christ, who shall come to judge the living and the dead, and the world by fire. Amen.

Let us pray. O God, who for the salvation of mankind has founded one of Thy greatest sacraments in the element of water, graciously give ear when we call upon Thee, and pour upon this element, prepared for diverse purifications, the power of Thy blessing; let Thy creature serving in Thy mysteries, by divine grace be effectual for casting out devils and for driving away diseases, that on whatsoever in the houses or places of the faithful this water shall be sprinkled, it may be freed from all uncleanness, and delivered from hurt. Let not the blast of pestilence nor disease remain there; let every enemy that lieth in wait depart; and if there be aught that hath ill will to the safety and quietness of the inhabitants, let it flee away at the sprinkling of this water, that they, being healed by the invocation of Thy holy name, may be defended from all that rise up against them. Through our Lord Jesus Christ, who in unity with Thee and the Holy Spirit liveth and reigneth forever. Amen.

The priest then mingles the salt with water in the form of a cross, saying:

Let this become a mixture of salt and water, in the name of the Father, and of the Son, and of the Holy Spirit. Amen.

The Lord be with you.

And with thy spirit.

Let us pray. O God, Author of invincible might, King of unconquerable dominion, and ever a Conqueror who doest wonders; who puttest down the strength of all that rise up against Thee; who overcomest the rage of the adversary; who by Thy power doest cast down his wickedness; we, O Lord, with fear and trembling, humbly entreat and implore Thee to mercifully look upon this creature of salt and water, to graciously illumine and sanctify it with the dew of Thy favor; that wheresoever it shall be sprinkled, by the invocation of Thy holy name, all troubling of unclean spirits may be cast out, and the dread of the poisonous serpent be chased far away: and let the presence of the Holy Spirit vouchsafe to be with us, who ask Thy mercy, in every place. Through our Lord Jesus Christ, who lives and reigns with Thee in unity with this same Holy Spirit forever. Amen.

From these beautiful prayers of sanctification it is plain that we can gain grace for body and soul.

Chapter 4

THE EFFECTS OF HOLY WATER

The question naturally presents itself: whence come the effects of holy water?

For the effects of holy water we are indebted principally to our divine Savior. He merited for us the graces we obtain through its usage by His bitter Passion and death. Holy Church, however, who is the custodian of these precious and infinite treasures of grace merited by our Lord, has, in view of these merits, attached these effects to holy water. The power for doing this she has from Christ Himself; hence we owe the effects of holy water primarily to Christ, and secondarily to the will and the prayers of the Church.

Concerning the effects, it is to be noted that, by holy water, sanctifying grace is not conferred, but actual grace is obtained, such grace, for instance, through which the intellect is enlightened and the will is moved to avoid evil and to do good. Corporal benefits also are obtained by holy water.

But if we wish to obtain great effects from the use of Holy Water, must we be correspondingly well prepared. To be thus prepared, we must above all be in the state of grace and have firm faith in and submission to Christ and His Holy Church. By this it must not be understood that to one even thus disposed, all the effects attached to the use of holy water will be granted, but we know that graces will be accorded to whoever takes holy water in the proper disposition. How many graces or favors one obtains cannot be determined.

Nor will one invariably obtain the good or the grace that he seeks to obtain through holy water however well he may be prepared.

For instance, holy water may be taken to relieve the subject from sickness. He takes it with firm faith and great confidence. Will he be cured without fail? No. On the contrary, however, he will invariably obtain some other grace that is equally as important to him, or more so.

But why does holy water not infallibly bring the desired effect, even though used with a proper disposition?

The *Catechism* teaches that the sacramentals, consequently holy water, operate principally by means of the Church's intercession (CCC 1667). The Church is the bride of the Divine Savior, and hence her prayers are always pleasing to God. When the Church prays, the divine bridegroom prays with her, and for this reason her prayer is powerful with God.

Thus it may happen that a lukewarm Christian may derive great benefit from the use of holy water. The reason for this is that God looks not on the unworthiness of mankind but rather on the prayer of the Church, so pleasing to Him. Especially, though, will the loyal children of the Church, who seek to coordinate their ideas to those of the divine Savior and of the Church, participate in the blissful effects of holy water.

Thus far, the effects of holy water have been considered in a general way; they shall now be treated of in detail.

These are, as previously stated, of a twofold nature: the effects of grace for the body and the effects of grace for the soul. Words used in the first prayer that the Church pronounces in blessing the salt are "that thou be to all who take thee salvation of soul and body," and in the second prayer, "let it be to all who take it, health of mind and body." Inasmuch as harmful influences, and sometimes sickness, originate largely with the devil, the prayer of the Church in the blessing of the water directs herself principally against the evil spirit, and consequently holy water is in an especial manner a means of protection against this evil spirit.

As we learn from these same prayers of the Church, holy water is a special remedy against ills of the body. This effect is contained in the second prayer pronounced over the water. Therein the Church thus addresses herself to God:

> Graciously give ear when we call upon Thee, and pour upon this element ... the power of Thy blessing; let Thy creature salt ... by divine grace be effectual for driving away diseases, that on whatsoever in the houses or places of the faithful this water shall be sprinkled, it may be freed from all uncleanness and be delivered from hurt.

From these words it is plain that holy water is not only a means to drive away sickness but is likewise a protection against sickness.

But Holy Church, in her prayer for the bodily welfare of her children, shows still more foresight. She knows well that not only corporal sufferings, but misfortune in temporal possessions as well, are painful to mankind.

Holy Church consequently offers a means of protection against such mishaps, when she implores in the second prayer over the water, "let not the blast of pestilence nor disease remain" where this water is sprinkled. All harmful influence of the elements, and the powers of the enemy, the Church wishes to keep from mankind, and hence she prays: "and if there be aught which hath ill will to the safety and quietness of the inhabitants, let it flee away at the sprinkling of this water."

"I have myself felt an extraordinary consolation when I have used holy water. It is certain that I have felt a great joy and inner peace which I cannot describe, a joy with which my soul was quite refreshed. This is not merely an effect of the imagination, nor a rare occurrence. I have experienced it frequently and paid special attention to it. On these occasions I feel like one who, suffering intense thirst, takes a glass of water and is quite refreshed.

From this we can see how important everything instituted by the Church is; it comforts me to see the great power which her blessing imparts to water, so great is the difference between blessed and unblessed water."

ST. TERESA OF ÁVILA
(1515–1582)

Thus holy water advances the bodily welfare of the faithful. A brief narrative will show us that it also achieves the advancement of the soul's welfare.

As the soul is far superior to the body, so too are the spiritual effects of holy water superior to the corporal effects. The prayers used in the blessing do not specify these spiritual effects; they speak only in general of the advancement of our soul's salvation through this holy water. For example, in the prayers that are said over the salt, the words occur, "be to all who take thee salvation of soul and body," and "health of mind and body."

In like manner the spiritual effect is expressed only in a general way in the concluding prayer, when the Church directs her petition to God that He may illumine and sanctify the salt and the water,

that wheresoever it shall be sprinkled,
by the invocation of Thy holy name
all troubling of unclean spirits may be
cast out, and the dread of the poisonous
serpent be chased far away; and let the
presence of the Holy Spirit vouchsafe to
be with us, who ask Thy mercy, in every
place.

In these words the petition is that holy water
may shield us against the influence of the evil
one — hence the purifying effect — and secure
for us assistance in the grace of the Holy Spirit,
wherein is expressed the sanctifying effect.

That holy water possesses this purifying and
sanctifying effect is indicated in the following
prayer used by the Church in its distribution:
"Thou shalt sprinkle me, O Lord, with hyssop,
and I shall be cleansed : Thou shalt wash me,
and I shall be made whiter than snow ... and

all unto whom that water came were saved." These words clearly point to a purifying and sanctifying effect of holy water. We may not, however, conclude from this that any purifying from mortal sin takes place, because none of the sacramentals cleanses from such sin; but we are correct in assuming a purifying from venial sin and from temporal punishments due to sin.

Doctors of the Church agree that holy water causes the remission of venial sin and of temporal punishment due to sin. I quote St. Thomas Aquinas: "By the sprinkling of holy water the debt of venial sin is wiped out; but not always, however, are all temporal punishments relinquished; this takes place in proportion to the disposition of the person using it, depending on the less or greater degree of ardor in the love for God on the part of the person using it."

"I was once in an oratory, and [the devil] appeared to me in an abominable form at my left side. It seemed that a great flame, all bright without shadow, came forth from his body. He told me in a terrifying way that I had really freed myself from his hands but that he would catch me with them again. I was struck with great fear and blessed myself as best I could; he disappeared, but returned right away. This happened to me twice. I didn't know what to do. There was some holy water there, and I threw it in that direction; he never returned again…. I often experience that there is nothing the devils flee from more—without returning—than holy water."

ST. TERESA OF ÁVILA

Again the same holy Doctor says that "the sprinkling of holy water brings about the remission of venial sin in the measure of which it excites to contrition." In accord with the advice of St. Alphonsus, one should strive when using holy water to rise to contrition, that it may prove its purifying effects.

Holy water not only possesses the power of cleansing us from venial sin and temporal punishments but also helps us to overcome the temptations of the devil. To bring about this effect, Holy Church asks in the first prayer pronounced over the salt that Almighty God may effect that it serve for the preservation of the people, that "every delusion and wickedness of the devil, and all unclean spirits, may fly and depart." Still more: in the second prayer over the salt, it shall even shield us against all assaults of spiritual wickedness; hence thus to protect us against temptation, that the devil may have even less power to tempt us.

Holy water also has sanctifying effects. These consist in the actual graces that may be obtained. These are illuminations of the intellect and inspirations of the Holy Spirit that aid the faithful to perform loyally the duties of their state of life, to pray devoutly, to hear a sermon with profit, and especially to assist with recollection and devotion at the Holy Sacrifice of Mass, and thus richly participate in its precious treasures. An illumination, for instance, may be involved when one comes to comprehend, better than he has known before, his faults and particularly his prevailing sin. An inspiration, however, is when an inward voice admonishes him to resolve finally to avoid the occasion of sin, to give up a sinful acquaintance, to shun bad associations or dangerous occasions, with greater determination, and to seek after, with a special devotion and earnestness, the virtue that is in opposition to his prevailing vice. These are effects of the actual graces, effects that holy water can bring about.

I do not maintain that the above-named or similar effects of grace must necessarily be attributed to the use of holy water, because we cannot know what and how much it has effected in us. But we do know that it can produce these effects, and we may without doubt have occasion to attribute much of our knowledge and inspiration to the use of holy water.

"St. Matthew ordained that the bishop should bless water or oil, as follows: Lord of Sabaoth, God of power, the Creator of water and giver of oil, Thou who pardonest and lovest man, Thou didst give water to drink and cleanse, and oil for gladness; vouchsafe, then, to sanctify this water and oil for Christ's sake: ... give to it the power of healing and expelling sickness, of driving away devils, and of rescuing from all snares, through Christ our hope. Amen."

APOSTOLIC CONSTITUTIONS
(CA. A.D. 380)

Chapter 5

❧ ——————————— ❧

The Use of Holy Water
by the Church

As holy water can accomplish so many effects for body and soul, it is easily understood why the Church should adapt its use in many ways in her divine service and likewise recommend its pious usage to the faithful. Its most solemn use by the Church is in the Asperges, in sprinkling the faithful, previous to the principal service of Sundays.

As the Lord's Prayer is denoted the Our Father because it begins with these words, so is the giving of holy water before the beginning of Sunday service styled Asperges, because the prayer that the priest offers in distributing holy water begins with the word *Asperges*. The hymn "Asperges me Domine hyssopo et mundabor, lavabis me, et super nivem dealbabor," reads in English, "Thou shalt sprinkle me, O Lord, with hyssop, and I shall be cleansed: Thou shalt wash me, and I shall be made whiter than snow."

According to the prescribed rule of the Church, holy water shall be given on Sunday only, and then just preceding the principal morning service. The priest to officiate at this service first sprinkles himself, then the altar, then the faithful. The altar is a symbol of Christ, but the priest is the mediator between Christ and the people. By this sprinkling of the altar and the people, expression is given to the idea that Christ and the faithful form a unit, that the people are members of the Mystical Body of Christ. So, then, the altar is the place where the Holy Sacrifice of the Mass, the unbloody offering of the New Testament, is presented and is therefore a place whence flow many graces for the faithful. Precisely this fullness of grace that the faithful receive is plainly typified because the priest goes from the altar, out among the people, to sprinkle them.

But because the priest, before beginning Holy Mass, sprinkles himself, the altar, and the faithful, there is therefore something else quite special to be attained. It is this: the priest, the altar, the faithful, shall become, as much as can be, clean and holy, for the worthy celebration of Holy Mass. No one indeed can say that he is too pure to offer, or to assist at, this Holy Sacrifice. And if in the Old Testament they who according to the law were unclean must first be purified by the sprinkling of the water of expiation, that they might become worthy to assist at the sacrificial acts, how much the more does the infinite sanctity of the sacrifice of the New Testament demand that all who assist thereat shall insofar as is possible become purified.

During the Easter season, instead of the Asperges, the Vidi Aquam is intoned. "Vidi aquam egredientem de templo a latere dextro, alleluia: et omnes, ad quos pervenit aqua ista, salvi facti sunt et dicent, alleluia, alleluia." Given in English: "I saw water flowing from the right side of the temple, Alleluia; and all to whom that water came were saved, and they shall say, Alleluia, alleluia."

The Vidi Aquam was chanted in the first centuries of the Christian era, but from emotions different from those of today. In those days it was sung by the newly baptized, who had received baptism on Holy Saturday. These daily walked in procession at Vespertide during the Easter week, to the baptismal font, and chanted, besides other anthems, the Vidi Aquam. As the Church intones this hymnal at Easter she desires to direct our mind to the water of holy baptism, and likewise to the water that flowed from the opened side of the divine Redeemer and also to the rich source of grace, from which at Easter all Christendom is bedewed with spiritual renewal, expiation, and sanctification. The alleluias of this canticle bring expression to the joy over the Resurrection of the divine Savior and find an echo in the soul of every believing Christian; for through holy baptism we, too, have spiritually risen with Christ.

As previously remarked, the Asperges preceding the principal Sunday service is the solemn ceremony through which holy water finds its application. In a less solemn manner the Asperges is applied on pastoral visits.

When the priest enters the room of the sick, he sprinkles the sick, and likewise the room, with holy water, meanwhile reciting the Asperges. By this sprinkling shall be banished any possible evil influence from the sick and from the dwelling.

The Church furthermore uses holy water in blessings and dedications, and indeed it is used in most of these. When, for example, the priest offers the blessing over the sick, he sprinkles him with holy water. When, as is the custom in some localities, wine is blessed on the feast of St. John the Evangelist, or bread on the feast of St. Agatha, or when incense is blessed on Epiphany, or ashes on Ash Wednesday, or palms on Palm Sunday, all these objects to be blessed are sprinkled with holy water.

Thus is holy water used in most blessings and dedications. In many of these it has a higher meaning than at first glance would appear. And this great significance consists in this: that by the sprinkling of holy water the object to be blessed receives the same power that rests in the holy water. These effects can be imparted by the priest or by any believer. If the priest imparts them, he does so in asking from God, in the

name of the Church, those particular effects
that he hopes for in the object blessed. If the
faithful perform the ceremony, then the effects
of holy water are merely transferred to the re-
ceiving object. The objects here considered are
either food or drink, medicines or like articles.

The Church uses holy water in funeral ceremonies. As every Catholic Christian knows
from his catechism, the Church Militant, the
Church Suffering, and the Church Triumphant
constitute the Communion of Saints, a mystical
body of which Christ is the head. The Church
Militant can aid the Church Suffering by her
intercession. This intercessory prayer may be
the offering of the Holy Sacrifice of the Mass,
the application of indulgences, good works, or
prayers, offered for the souls in purgatory.

When the Church sprinkles holy water
in funeral ceremonies, her prayerful hope
and wish is symbolized: that the soul of the

departed may be expiated and sanctified for
the great Day of Judgment. To make this hope
effective the Church joins the sprinkling with
a prayer. When the priest receives the corpse,
having sprinkled the coffin with holy water,
he recites Psalm 129 (RSV = Ps. 130). In this
psalm the abiding hope is expressed that the
deceased may find mercy with God, and at its
conclusion the petition is added, "Eternal rest
grant unto him, O Lord, and let perpetual light
shine upon him."

And while the priest three times sprinkles
the body when lowered into the grave, he prays,
"May the soul be refreshed in the Heavenly
Kingdom by the Almighty God, the Father, the
Son, and the Holy Spirit. Amen."

And how impressive the prayer of the
Church, as at the coffin she prays in the name of
the deceased, before sprinkling the holy water:
"Deliver me, O Lord, from eternal death in that

awful day: when the heavens and the earth shall be shaken: when Thou shalt come to judge the world by fire." And while the priest sprinkles the holy water, he recites the Our Father.

As the dew refreshes the flowers that have been exposed to the rays of the sun, so holy water, the heavenly dew, conjoined with prayer, refreshes the souls in purgatory and lessens their sufferings. In the Gospel, Dives, suffering in hell, asked in vain that Abraham but dip a finger into water and cool his parching tongue (Luke 16:24). His wish was not granted. Hell is barred by the justice of God so that no mercy can enter there. In purgatory, however, mercy still has an entrance. Holy Church, our Mother, dips her blessing hand into the sanctified water to soothe the burning pains of the suffering souls.

The Church applies holy water in funeral ceremonies not only to aid the soul of the departed, but likewise for the sake of the lifeless body. This body was a temple of the Holy Spirit, the bearer of an immortal soul, which will be again united on the last day. The Church consequently sanctifies the corruptible corpse that it may be the more worthy to become an incorruptible body unto resurrection, to be forever the dwelling place of the soul. For the same reason the corpse of a child is sprinkled with holy water, and likewise also is the grave blessed. Thus is enhanced the dignity of the corpse that is bedded to rest in a home of earth. At the same time this occurs, too, to keep from the grave any influence of Satan.

Chapter 6

THE USE OF HOLY WATER
BY THE FAITHFUL

We have studied how the Church makes use of holy water. But it is her earnest wish that the faithful likewise make pious and fervent use of this means of grace. She therefore on every Sunday, excepting Easter and Pentecost Sundays, in those churches where baptismal water was blessed on the previous day, blesses water and keeps it in a place and vessel especially adapted for this purpose. From this the faithful can, and should, carry it to their homes. In keeping with this, the Roman Ritual admonishes the faithful to take some of the blessed water with them and to sprinkle the sick, the homes, and the fields. And, too, they should keep it in their apartments and frequently during the day sprinkle themselves with it. In the church edifice the faithful are offered an opportunity to participate in the sanctifying effects of holy water, for in every church there is at least one holy-water vessel from which the people upon entering and leaving the building may take holy water.

Holy water should awaken a contrite disposition in the faithful on entering the church, that they may appear in God's presence with a pure heart. And then shall the mind be purified of worldly thoughts, which so greatly disturb devotion and recollection in prayer. The faithful should herein follow the example of St. Stephen, the third Abbot of Citeaux, whose biographers relate that upon entering the church he was wont to close the door after him and say, "You thoughts of worldly affairs, remain outside and await my return. I have no use of you now, as I have an important task to perform. My time is now entirely taken up with God."

These thoughts should likewise fill the hearts of the faithful when, on entering the church, they take holy water.

On leaving the church, they should join with the sprinkling of holy water a prayer to God that He would guard the good thoughts and strengthen the good resolutions formed during divine services.

Thus Holy Church plainly shows her endeavor to gain the beneficial effects of holy water for the faithful, who on their part should enter into this spirit of Mother Church and not only take holy water in the house of worship but should often use it in their dwellings, and consequently it should also be found in every Catholic home. With every family there should be a well-filled holy water vase, and every member of the family should enjoy the opportunity it affords. It is a beautiful and praiseworthy custom to take holy water when rising in the morning and when retiring at night.

When a new day dawns, who will say what it may bring with it? Who can foretell the dangers that may await the life of the body, or the more precious life of the soul? Since the Christian, even if he be in the state of sanctifying grace, has much to lose, it is certainly a measure of prudence to use every means at his disposal to guard against any loss of this precious treasure.

We have no doubt sufficiently indicated that holy water is precisely a special safeguard against all dangers. What! If with a drop of holy water one makes the Sign of the Cross upon his forehead, he can banish the roaring lion, the devilish enemy, is it not worthwhile in time of temptation to use holy water?

And again: If the believing Christian considers what dangers he may encounter when entering the mining shaft, or ascending to the burning oven, serving at the machines in the great factories, traveling on railways or steamships, he ought be glad, every morning, to make use of Holy Water that he may share in the blessings and prayers of Holy Church.

Many dangers likewise threaten the children, dangers to body and soul. The child is inexperienced and does not dream of danger. Oftentimes parents are careless or haven't the time or opportunity to guard their children sufficiently. And how numerous, too, are the dangers for the soul of the child. It becomes almost impossible for parents alone to ward these off entirely from their children. Unfortunately there are too many of the enemy who seek to sow the seed of wrong in the heart of the innocent child.

What better can parents do who are concerned about the welfare of their children than to recommend them to God's protection and

to the care of their guardian angel, to which
act we would direct especial attention — what
better can they do than to give them holy water
and gradually lead them to its use, that by this
means they share in the prayers of the Church,
and thus safely place them against the influences of the demon and the manifold dangers
to body and soul?

Not only in broad daylight, but even in darkness, is mankind threatened with dangers. Man
may rest, but the devil, never.

At night, and particularly at night, the devil
plans ruin to the soul of man. When the pious
Christian is about to lay himself to rest, and
with holy water marks his forehead, his lips,
and his heart, he well may earnestly plead with
God to shield him against the delusions of the
devil.

For this indeed does the Church pray in her
blessings that "every delusion and wickedness of

the devil depart" by virtue of holy water. Consequently, one will take holy water at eventide to cleanse the soul from the venial sins of the passing day, as also to rest secure for the night against the onslaughts of the evil spirit.

It is well also to suggest that holy water is a wholesome remedy for the sick. Let them who nurse the sick be concerned that they have opportunity to use holy water, nor let the sick neglect often to sprinkle themselves with it, being mindful of the prayers of the Church, that holy water may possess the power of driving away sickness. Convinced of this, the invalid cannot too often take advantage of the opportunity given. He may likewise sprinkle in the manner of a cross the medicinal remedies to be used. When the patient suffers, and is in misery from pain, let him use it with confidence and prayer.

When the death struggle approaches and the demon redoubles his efforts, then especially should the patient be frequently sprinkled with the sanctified water, mindful that Holy Church implores in her prayers and blessings against the onslaughts of the devil. The Church especially advises that holy water should be carried to the home in order to sprinkle the sick.

Not alone man, but whatever stands in relation to him, shall by the use of holy water be protected against the power of the destroying angel of wickedness. It is therefore the desire of Holy Church that the faithful sprinkle holy water in their houses and on their fields, to keep away damaging influences and to intercede for the fruitfulness of their acres. For these effects does the Church in her blessings thus implore: "that on whatsoever in the houses or in the places of the faithful this water shall be sprinkled, it may be freed from all uncleanness and delivered from hurt. Let not the blast of pestilence nor disease remain there; and if there be aught that hath ill will to the safety and quiet of the inhabitants, let it flee away at the sprinkling of this water."

From what has been said it is easy to observe how manifold are the effects of holy water. We cannot at once grasp all these effects nor have them in view at the moment of using it. If we, however, aim to use it with devotion and confidence, we may confidently hope that God will have us share in precisely those effects that will be most beneficial for our bodily and spiritual welfare, even though at the time we had no thought of these.

As Mother Church gives holy water to her deceased members, so is it her wish that the faithful should give it to their departed. Therefore, it is a genuine Catholic custom for the faithful, as is the case in many places when assisting at the "death watch," to sprinkle the corpse with holy water and also to perform the same pious act when visiting a cemetery, to sprinkle the grave with holy water.

Nor should there be omission at the same time to pray for the suffering souls, which is in accord with the examples of Holy Church; for instance, "Eternal rest grant unto them, O Lord, and let perpetual light shine upon them. May they rest in peace. Amen." Thus holy water becomes a sort of heavenly dew that refreshes the souls in purgatory and soothes their sufferings.

CONCLUSION

We have briefly shown the significance of holy water, which it possesses in the sanctifying order. The believing Christian knows well that it is not sufficient merely to take or use holy water to make secure of its effects, but that it is necessary to avoid sin, and the occasions of sin, to keep God's commands, to make use of the means of grace, and to lead a pious Christian life.

From the above conclusions, it is plain that holy water is likewise to be appreciated as an aid to further the temporal and spiritual welfare of man. Hence there should not be any further need of encouragement for the earnest Christian to make frequent use of it; he is encouraged to do so by the thought that our divine

Savior, by the spilling of His precious blood, has merited the graces of which, through this blessed water, we may become participants.

He is also encouraged by the fact that our Holy Mother, the Church, who is so earnestly desirous of the welfare of her children, wishes that we persistently use it. Finally, he is encouraged to do this by the consideration of the effects of holy water for both body and soul. Could it be possible that an earnest Catholic would close his ears to this threefold incentive? Surely not. Rather would his debt of love and gratitude to the divine Savior and to the Church, as well as his anxiety for his own corporal and spiritual welfare, be an incentive to him, cheerfully often, and with confidence and devotion to make use of holy water.

Let us follow the admonition of the Holy Spirit: "You shall draw water with joy out of the Savior's fountains" (Isa. 12:3).

APPENDICES

Appendix A

―――――――――――

QUESTIONS AND
ANSWERS

How ancient is the use of holy water in the Catholic Church?

As most all doctrines and ordinances of the Catholic Church have been subjected to antagonism and scorn, so has holy water been the subject of attack upon the Church. It has been charged that the Church brought about the use of holy water in the later centuries. Against these attacks be it remarked: the prayers and ceremonies by which water is blessed, are, as may readily be perceived, so serious and elevated, their significance so great, that only a malicious disposition would trifle with such means of grace.

As concerns the use of holy water, it is undoubtedly very ancient. In a writing bearing the title *Apostolic Constitutions*, composed at the very latest in the year 400, there is mention of a blessed water effective for the protection of health, the healing of the sick, the keeping away of demons and all that is evil, the same as the holy water of the present day.

Without any doubt, however, the use of such a sacramental in the Church is still more ancient. Furthermore, the prayers that the priest uses at present in blessing water, which have been quoted, are found in our exact wording in a book written by Pope St. Gregory the Great (who died in 604).

Is holy water an innovation by the Church?

We have already stated that holy water is a sacramental, and that the sacramentals were ordained not by Christ but by the Catholic

Church through the authority of Christ. Christ said to the Supreme Head of the Church, "Amen, I say to you, whatsoever you shall bind upon earth shall be bound also in heaven, and whatsoever you shall loose upon earth shall be loosed also in heaven" (Matt. 18:18).

The Church consequently could ordain the use of holy water at any time according to her pleasure, as she could also discontinue it if she deemed it advisable or necessary. Holy Church, therefore, merely exercised her prerogative or right in establishing the use of holy water.

In the Asperges, do those whom the holy water does not reach participate in its effects?

Another question that arises here concerns especially the Asperges before the principal Sunday service. When the holy water is distributed, it is quite probable that many of the faithful are not reached by it. These, to some extent, are therefore of the opinion that they do not share in its distribution. This fear is without foundation. For even if they are not reached by it, they can nevertheless participate in its effects, if they are desirous of participation, and manifest this desire by some outward sign; for instance, by rising, by bowing the head, or making upon themselves the Sign of the Cross.

In like manner it is not necessary, in the blessing of the palms on Palm Sunday, or the blessing of herbs on the feast of the Assumption of the Blessed Virgin, that each palm or each herb be reached or touched by the holy water, but it is sufficient that the priest conducting the ceremony have the intention to bless the palms or objects placed before him, which is, of course, always the case.

If the holy water at hand might not be sufficient for the occasion, may water that is not blessed be added?

Yes. But care must be taken not to add as great a quantity as there is of holy water.

How can I use holy water in my home?

Your local Catholic gift shop offers many holy-water fonts for the home. Place one on the wall in a regularly used hallway or near your front door. Carry a clean vessel to your parish church and fill it from the large holy-water container there. If you cannot find it, just ask the priest, who will be thrilled that you want some to carry home with you. Store your holy water in vessels that you have labeled "holy water" or in decorative bottles made for that purpose, also sold by Catholic gift shops.

Use the water as you do in church, dipping your fingers into it, and making the Sign of the

Cross. Bless your children with it at night, using your thumb to make the Sign of the Cross with holy water on their foreheads.

Appendix B

❦———————————————❦

EIGHT WAYS TO USE
HOLY WATER IN YOUR
EVERYDAY LIFE

by Gretchen Filz

1. Bless yourself.

If we bless ourselves with holy water only on Sundays, aren't we missing out on the rest of the week? You can never have too much grace or blessing in your life. Use holy water daily. Keeping a holy-water font in your home is a great idea so that you, your family, and your guests can be blessed in your comings and goings. Keep the font by the front door to ensure that you never leave home without it. See Appendix C for prayers to use in blessing yourself.

2. Bless your house.

If you haven't taken the time to bless your house with holy water, then no time is better than the present. Your home is a domestic church and is in need of spiritual protection. You can sprinkle holy water in your home yourself or have a priest formally bless your home using holy water as part of the blessing ceremony.

3. Bless your family.

Use holy water to pray and make the Sign of the Cross over your spouse and children before they go to sleep at night. Bonding the family to each other and to God in this way is a great family tradition to adopt. Keep a bottle of holy water at your bedside for this purpose

4. Bless your work space.

Sprinkling your work space with holy water is a great idea, not only for spiritual protection in your workplace but also as to sanctify your daily work for the glory of God

5. Bless your car.

The car is probably the most dangerous place where you spend a significant amount of time daily. Never underestimate the power of holy water applied to your vehicle to keep you safe from harm's way, when used in faith and trust in God.

6. Bless your vegetable garden.

It was a common practice in the Middle Ages for people to sprinkle their vegetable gardens with holy water. In times when people were very dependent on crops for their livelihood, lack of rain or early frosts could be devastating. Using holy water to bless and sanctify the plants that would be used for the family's sustenance showed their reliance on God's grace.

7. Bless the sick.

Blessing sick family members or friends with holy water probably counts as a corporeal and a spiritual work of mercy. If you visit the sick in a hospital or a nursing home, bless their living space with holy water as well and leave a bottle of it with them as a comfort in their time of need.

8. Bless your pets.

Many parishes have a rite of blessing for pets on the feast of St. Francis of Assisi. Pets are beloved companions for individuals and families and often provide a great service to them, and even these can be blessed with holy water because all creation has the end of giving glory to God. This also applies to livestock and farm animals that provide labor, livelihood, and nourishment to humans.

Holy Water is one of those beautiful gifts (and weapons) from God to keep us sanctified and holy in our daily lives and to keep the things we regularly use sanctified and holy. Let us stop and think of what a generous gift holy water is for us, so that we will use it more frequently, thoughtfully, and gratefully![2]

---

[2] "Eight Ways to Use Holy Water in Your Everyday Life" is reprinted with permission from the August 12, 2014, blog post on *GetFed*, sponsored by the Catholic Company: https://www.catholiccompany.com/getfed/8-ways-to-use-holy-water/.

Appendix C

Prayers for Blessing Yourself with Holy Water

Make the Sign of the Cross
while blessing yourself with holy water
and saying:

"IN THE NAME OF THE FATHER,
AND OF THE SON,
AND OF THE HOLY SPIRIT."

Make the Sign of the Cross
while blessing yourself with holy water
and saying:

"BY THY PRECIOUS BLOOD
AND BY THIS HOLY WATER,
CLEANSE ME FROM MY SINS,
O LORD."

Make the Sign of the Cross
while blessing yourself with holy water
and saying:

"SWEET HEART OF JESUS,
GRANT THAT I MAY LOVE THEE
MORE AND MORE."

Make the Sign of the Cross
while blessing yourself with holy water
and saying:

"SWEET HEART OF MARY,
BE MY SALVATION."

Make the Sign of the Cross
while blessing yourself with holy water
and saying:

"JESUS, MARY, JOSEPH,
I GIVE YOU MY HEART
AND MY SOUL."

Make the Sign of the Cross
while blessing yourself with holy water
and saying:

"JESUS, MARY, JOSEPH,
ASSIST ME IN MY LAST AGONY."

Make the Sign of the Cross
while blessing yourself with holy water
and saying:

"JESUS, MARY, JOSEPH,
MAY MY SOUL DEPART
IN PEACE WITH YOU."

Make the Sign of the Cross
while blessing yourself with holy water
and saying:

"MY JESUS, MERCY."

Make the Sign of the Cross
while blessing yourself with holy water
and saying:

"PRAISED BE JESUS CHRIST."

Sophia Institute

Sophia Institute is a nonprofit institution that seeks to nurture the spiritual, moral, and cultural life of souls and to spread the Gospel of Christ in conformity with the authentic teachings of the Roman Catholic Church.

Sophia Institute Press fulfills this mission by offering translations, reprints, and new publications that afford readers a rich source of the enduring wisdom of mankind.

Sophia Institute also operates two popular online Catholic resources: CrisisMagazine.com and CatholicExchange.com.

Crisis Magazine provides insightful cultural analysis that arms readers with the arguments necessary for navigating the ideological and theological minefields of the day. *Catholic Exchange* provides world news from a Catholic perspective as well as daily devotionals and articles that will help you to grow in holiness and live a life consistent with the teachings of the Church.

In 2013, Sophia Institute launched Sophia Institute for Teachers to renew and rebuild Catholic culture through service to Catholic education. With the goal of nurturing the spiritual, moral, and cultural life of souls, and an abiding respect for the role and work of teachers, we strive to provide materials and programs that are at once enlightening to the mind and ennobling to the heart; faithful and complete, as well as useful and practical.

Sophia Institute gratefully recognizes the Solidarity Association for preserving and encouraging the growth of our apostolate over the course of many years. Without their generous and timely support, this book would not be in your hands.

www.SophiaInstitute.com
www.CatholicExchange.com
www.CrisisMagazine.com
www.SophiaInstituteforTeachers.org